Southern Steam Days Remembered II

Strathwood

Southern Steam Days Remembered II

Front Cover: Our driver for the Bournemouth line express to depart behind 35018 British India Line, stands back to admire his steed, perhaps happier than if he were rostered, 34087 145 Squadron, instead. Both will shortly head off through the maze of lines here at Waterloo and head for the former LSWR mainline to the south coast resort on 26 October, 1963. *Strathwood Library Collection*

Strathwood

Southern Steam Days
Remembered II

First published 2017
ISBN 1-905276-52-4
ISBN 978-1-905276-52-3

Published by Strathwood Publishing, 9 Boswell Crescent, Inverness, IV2 3ET
Telephone 01463 234004

Printed by Akcent Media

Contents

Page

Preface

Thankful that the first volume in this Steam Days Remembered series was so well received at its launch during the Eastleigh Works Open Day in 2009, this second and third volume released together are perhaps well overdue, after such a wait.

It was planned to release this second volume a number of years ago, so to those of you who have been patiently waiting for its release with kind words of encouragement, I thank you. The release of both this and the third volume at the same time is to commemorate the fact that fifty years have passed since the demise of regular Southern Region steam in the summer of 1967. As a young school boy at the time living close to Feltham my recollections of this final gasp of the dying steam railway are made all the clearer by the wonderful photographs, thankfully recording this era. Not to mention those who were involved, such as my old friend Roger Carrell, and all of those who have taken the time and trouble, to set down on paper some of their wonderful tales and experiences from this sadly missed time.

Roger and myself made our acquaintance over thirty years ago on the other side of the world from our beloved Southern Region in Western Australia. Through the wonders of email we remain in touch to this day within a close group of friends across the globe who share a passion for British Railways steam.

We will all have our favourites from the past, I hope you will enjoy this compilation and we must also thank the foresight of the photographers and the kindness of those who have allowed their work to be seen and appreciated by a wider audience.

Kevin Derrick
Inverness 2017

Below: This would be Urie H16, 30520's last overhaul visit to Eastleigh Works in 1961 for all five of these impressive beasts from 70B Feltham would be withdrawn together in November, 1962. *Colour Rail*

Introduction - Working the Up Torrington to Feltham

After transferring from Nine Elms to Basingstoke MPD during late autumn 1963, I was delighted with a complete reversal from the high ratio of prep, and disposal duties at the former depot, to predominantly, main line running at the latter. In addition, there were more routes radiating from Basingstoke – effectively, to all points of the compass.

One duty I particularly enjoyed was the Up Torrington Goods to Feltham Yard – booked 02:40 hrs off Basingstoke. 'Enjoyment', at such a deathly hour of the night, only dawning into consciousness after arrival at work; having aroused from a deep-sleep at 01:30 and ventured-out into a bitterly-cold blackness to cycle three miles from home to the shed.

My permanent driver, Harold Dory and I book on at 02:20 hrs, read the relevant notices then make a can of tea. We exchange banter and pleasantries with the 'spare' crews then exit the warmth of our enginemen's cabin and make our way westward, to relieve Salisbury men shunting our train in the Up Yard.

The sight of ex works Bulleid Pacifics ready for a return to traffic at Eastleigh gained the attentions of many photographers, thankfully 34014 Budleigh Salterton on 25 April, 1963 was no exception. *Colour Rail*

The loco, at this period, is generally a Standard Class 5, either one of our named examples or a 'blow-in' cascaded from another region. Tonight it's 73082 Camelot, a Nine Elms based example. Directly behind the engine are a few cattle trucks containing an assortment of beasts that are, by now, somewhat restless due to their objections with the to-ing and fro-i-ing, and inevitable jolts, from shunting activities.

As we approach and sight the moving trucks, momentarily illuminated under a yard lamp, previous experience dictates that it's prudent to slow our pace in the hope that the last movement would be over by the time we arrive – the stench from frightened animals which engulfs the footplate during a reversal has to be experienced to be believed! Besides, it's unsafe to board an engine on the move and better to let seasoned 'rural' men cope with such aromas than us 'suburban' types!

Once on board and enjoying the radiance from the open firehole, the engine's assessments are given some attention - with one ear upon the fireman's report and the other upon the driver's – both being equally important. Following this the usual pleasantries are exchanged followed by the Salisbury men climbing down into the cold blackness of the night.

It's now 02:35 hrs, there's a good depth of bright fire, the needle's on 200 lb/sq in. with half a glass of water – ideal for keeping her quiet at such an inhospitable hour. Our guard appears on the nearside to give Harold the train's details; "Forty-three on with ten fitted!" is all I catch while I busy myself pouring two mugs of tea. We've got the dummy and the guard tells us to pull on out to save him walking back the whole length of the train!

We ease out onto the Up Local at about 5 mph. Having half closed the firehole doors, I saunter over to the nearside to hold up a steady white light facing rearward. As we approach the Up Local Platform the guard's swinging lamp is spotted in the rear and I acknowledge this with a similar repeat. Returning to my seat, I spot the Up Starting Gantry signalling us onto the Up Main, which I convey to Harold who responds by opening the regulator a little more. We're off!

With our train having now crossed-over and gently accelerating, we're up to 25 mph by the advanced starter, the darkness of the night gradually engulfing us as the lights of Basingstoke recede behind. It's downhill most of the way until we turn off at Byfleet (now Byfleet & New Haw!) so I build-up a large fire to take us there. As we touch 45 mph, Harold adjusts the reverser back to 20% and eases the regulator to maintain this speed; nothing for me to do now but sit down, roll a smoke and play with one injector – enjoyment indeed!

By Hook, with both having got a feel for our steed, we've migrated into our own little worlds. The rhythmic dong-dong - dong-dong-dong of a 4-6-0's wheels upon rail joints plus the regular hiss-hiss from cylinder glands have hypnotised us into a dreamlike state of forgotten memories and future hopes, while

Another visit in 1963 to the works yard at Eastleigh brings us 34084, 253 Squadron ready to take on whatever she would be called upon.
Strathwood Library Collection

we relax within the cosiness of this delightful sanctum. Winchfield, formally Shapley Heath – once an extremity of the old London and Southampton Railway - is passed with us barely noticing it, save from a dull pilot lamp.

Fleet comes and goes next, after which we're aroused with anticipation as we search ahead into the darkness for a spectacular highlight to an otherwise (hopefully) uneventful journey. As we approach Farnborough, we spot the Down Papers - rostered for a Merchant Navy at her head and, tonight, running a little late, as she bursts from under the road bridge and leans to the curve through the station, fireworks shooting high into the night sky from her Lemaitre chimney.

She then settles onto the straight, seemingly coming directly at us, volcanic larva ricocheting from carriage roofs and tumbling to the ground. I instinctively close my window and the firehole doors then vacate my seat as if to get out of her way!

This dramatic spectacle, appearing to be gaining speed as it approaches, finally roars past with a tremendous suck of air and a blur from lit carriage windows, barely three feet from where I'm standing and, as fast as it had appeared, it was gone - likewise swallowed-up by the darkness of the night, just like ourselves.

I'm now alert enough to return our 'office' to normal and find the motivation for some precautionary measures: having a nicely tuned live steam injector singing merrily, I turn on the tender coal sprays then look back along the train for any signs of smouldering fires; hoping the guard is doing the same from his own lonely sanctum!

In total contrast to what had passed before, we meekly lean to the left hand curve through Farnborough Station and under the road bridge. Next comes Sturt Lane Junction, where we pass over the Guildford - Reading line. Here, my mate winds her up to 30% and gives her a bit

Eastleigh's painters have made a splendid job on the lined green paintwork to Standard Class 5MT, 73049 on 15 September, 1963. Although it seems a little more work might be desireable around the smoke box number. *RCTS Collection*

On 9 September, 1962 it was the turn of 35016 Elders Fyffes to fly the flag outside at Eastleigh, whilst looking immaculate at the nearby shed. *Gerald T. Robinson*

Brookwood – which in days past served several military camps and the old Necropolis Company's private station at the Cemetery where Dugald Drummond was laid to rest. No sign of Drummy waving his fists tonight; we're certainly not working this 'contemporary' hard; besides, there's only one of his T9s left in active service and, what remains of his fleet of reliable M7s are working out their last days further west.

We'd drifted back to 25 mph to take the crossover onto the Up Local line and now we're back to 'offs' all the way as we gently accelerate back to 45 on the drop past St John's towards Woking. It's now 03:30 hrs and, as if Harold was psychic, we find ourselves converging with a 4-COR unit off the Guildford line on the approaches to Woking. I take the opportunity to peer into the windows of the naval train and . . . observe dead sailors everywhere!

The 4-COR unit quickly gains speed and overtakes us as we both shatter the night-time tranquillity of Woking station. I roll a smoke and fill the cab with the aroma of Old Holborn in anticipation that I'll have to start working the shovel when we depart the main line soon.

more stick before we dive into one of the short tunnels carrying the old Basingstoke Canal overhead. That threaded, we're now climbing slightly through Deepcut and she needs the extra power to dig us out of it and around the next curve past the notable Milepost 31 – which heralds the end of the steepest climb from the Thames Estuary.

Onward we trundle under the Farnham Up flyover and, having dropped to 40 mph through Deepcut, Harold returns the reverser and regulator to their previous settings knowing that we'll return to 45 mph on the steeper falling gradients through Brookwood.

I spot something amiss with the Outer Home as we approach Brookwood – the Distant is on! I call over to Harold who responds with, "Seen it!" He shuts off and gives the vacuum brake a tickle down to 15 inches (Water Gauge). Further on, the home gantry has signalled us onto the Up Local. Harold calls over, "Keeping us out of the way of some naval stuff from Pompey, I expect!"

We're barely out of Woking when Harold shuts off and lets her coast for the last few miles to the junction. We'll need to get down to 20 mph in order to take the severe Addlestone curve in safety, after which there's a testy climb up through Chertsey and Virginia Water.

Harold begins to play with the vacuum brake, so I take this as my cue to pick up the shovel and re-make another deep fire. We're down to 20 mph as we clonk through Byfleet and onto the sharp curve. Suddenly the whole train comes to life as it screams and squeals its objections in response to flange-torture, especially our engine!

Our line drops, levelling out where the Down line diverges, then climbs to gain the final straight; so halfway around the curve we have to apply power again! From here on my attention is focussed internally - maintaining my fire and water level for the engine's extra requirements – while externally, it's pitch dark!

We power through Addlestone station and on up through Chertsey, then onto the severe right hand curve through Virginia Water - which requires full power from our 'legendary castle' to keep our train moving. Finally, an easing-off and a welcome cessation to firing as we trundle along the easier grades past the reservoirs through Egham and Staines and onward to Ashford, while straining to recognise the various designs, from their lights, of aircraft beginning their approach to what must have been only an embryonic airport in 1964 compared to what Heathrow is today.

We cautiously trundle into Feltham Yard at 04:20 hrs and draw our train forward towards the Marshalling Tower and shunter's cabin. Upon coming to a stand via a "Whoa!" from the shunter, I hop down to uncouple and place a tail lamp on the tender, remembering not to get too close to the green runny stuff oozing from the front cattle wagon! Off to shed we chuff, where we'll vacate our engine to a disposal crew; thence to their messroom for 'breakfast' sandwiches and a can of fresh tea.

Our return trip usually involves boarding a prepared engine, (of any vintage!), and running light-engine, tender-first, to Clapham Carriage Sidings where we're booked to collect a parcels train and run down the Main-Line back to Basing'. The return is generally a doddle, although in winter time, running tender first in the cold and dark on a 'U Boat', 'S15' or similar, is no engineman's idea of comfort! A 'Charlie', Std 4 or 5MT would be much better.

But there's a pleasant surprise in store; while Harold and I insult each other over a game of cards, the Running Foreman pops in to give us 92231 for our return journey! Our new charge must be one of a handful of 9Fs cascaded to Feltham from Eastleigh when the Cromptons took over the Fawley – Bromford Bridge tanker trains, and this would be my first (but not last) trip on one.

We're due off shed in 10 minutes so we collect our gear and saunter stiffly outside into the bleak twilight of a cloudy dawn . . . to be greeted by a 9F in surprisingly pristine condition! I stow my gear, do a quick check of water level, fire and tools, then drop down and proceed to the front to check

our tail lamp and tightness of the smokebox door. Finally, to the back of the tender to check our headcode lamps and water level. While up on the tender, the coal is checked and trimmed for safety.

With everything correct and the coal dampened down, we back down towards the exit dummy and phone box. I give the bobby, "Light engine to Clapham Yard," and he pulls off for us immediately. We trundle out onto the mainline at 05:35 hrs; there's not much electric traffic around yet, a fact supported by a series of 'off' semaphores ahead of us. (Author's note: Steam engines never travelled 'forwards' or 'backwards', always 'chimney-first' or 'bunker/tender-first'.)

Without the warmth of the boiler ahead of us the draught blowing into the cab is quite bitter. The 'beat' from the wheels is distinctively different to anything I've experienced before and, although the cab is jolting vertically at each rail joint, the ride is very comfortable laterally. However, six-wheeled tenders never fail to amaze me with their tendency to crab

Whilst some of the Standard Class 5MTs were to be seen in green, sadly none of the Southern's named examples went this way, as demonstrated by 73089 Maid of Astolat. Sadly this fair maid would never look so good again. *Strathwood Library Collection*

from side to side, seemingly upon the centre axle, at every opportunity. I'd witnessed this many times when delivering and collecting Bulleid Pacifics and Standard classes between Waterloo and Nine Elms. Thus, while the engine is directionally steady, the tender isn't!

Through sleepy Twickenham and Richmond we sail at 40 mph, thence into neat, business-like Barnes - where the Brentford line converges with ours. It's all four-aspect colour-light signalling from here on so, no longer hindering Harold's sightings from the glare of the fire reflecting upon the tender front, I try my hand at some firing. The reach from shovelling plate to firehole is good and the firebox is the same shape as a Bulleid Pacific, but one peculiar thing is the shallowness of the grate – a design necessity to clear the rear driving axle, I surmise.

Putney appears out of the gloom after which we see a double yellow aspect. Harold shuts-off, on goes the blower slightly followed by the live-injector. We see a series of single yellows, and just beyond Clapham Junction station, a 'red' brings us to a stand just beyond Clapham Junction's 'A' Box. We hear the whirring of crossover switches followed by a clank from our 'dummy'. We edge, chimney-first, across the Down Windsor lines and cautiously enter the yard; a shunter stands ready to point to our train while calling that it's OK to run down this clear road and couple-up at the other end.

We clonk past our train of vans and come to a stand just before the double slips at the bottom of the yard. I hop down and set the road; the signal beyond.

Below: Having arrived at 71B Bournemouth three months beforehand after a short spell on LBSC metals at 75A Brighton, Drummond's Class M7, 30110 was back among friends once again working on the former LSWR at Wareham in July 1961 with the Swanage branch service. Note how the poor fireman is up to his waist in coal in the bunker, whilst the driver reads some notices. *Colour Rail*

then, once our engine has safely negotiated these and reached the buffer stops, I set the train-road for its reversal. Harold manoeuvres onto the train while I take a morning stroll in that direction.

When I reach the engine, he's hopped down for a feel around – she's a bit of a novelty for him too! I couple-up and remove my lamps from the tender rear, set my 'mainline' headcode, (Eastleigh have thoughtfully welded a bracket to the left side of the smokebox door!) then return to the warmth of the cab to put fire and water right ready for our departure. I hear voices and notice our guard deliberating with Harold on the ground. I catch, "Five bogies plus one CCT!" – something for our 9F to play with on the way home! The guard then calls up to me, "I've cracked-open the tap at the back, if you can s-p-a-r-e some steam!" With a loud guffaw he returns to the confines of his chosen abode - a MK1 BG - while I have a little guffaw of my own - the 9Fs don't have train heating!

About fifteen minutes later, there's a whistle from our guard in the rear prompting us to see a shunter way off in the distance gesturing us to set back. As we clear the confines of carriage stock on adjacent roads, I see that the dummy is off to set back onto the carriage-washing road between the Windsor and West of England mainlines. That manoeuvre performed, we stand behind another dummy awaiting a path down the mainline.

It's 06:15 hrs and early morning commuter traffic is increasing on all three routes that converge on Clapham Junction. Strictly speaking, we're not awaiting a path west but, rather, the opportunity to cross the Up SW Main Line and gain the Down Main. A 3-set 2-BIL EMU rushes past towards Waterloo; a few moments later our dummy clanks 'off'. A brief toot on the whistle and we set off to gain our path home.

It's been a bit of a challenge - getting both my boiler up to running conditions and keeping her quiet at the same time, particularly when the exact 'right-away' time isn't predictable.

Having negotiated the crossovers and gained the Down Main, Harold opens her up around the curve of the station. The blast from her chimney is solid and beautifully rhythmic, the volume of which isn't comprehended until it echoes back to us from the station buildings.

Once under the bridge at the west-end of the station, it's a steady climb to Earlsfield, thence upon level-ish ground towards Wimbledon. As we should have expected from a Class 9 with five foot drivers, she's accelerating away from Clapham as if running Light-Engine! With 25% cut-off and 1/4 regulator, we're up to 50 mph by Earlsfield, then things are eased as we touch the maximum urban limit of 60 mph by Durnsford Road.

The exhilaration from this interesting exercise is, however, short-lived - as we pass beneath the Up Local flyover, I spot a double-yellow at the Wimbledon home signal. Harold tickles the blower valve, shuts-off and both safety valves lift . . . all the way through the station and under the bridge at the west-end! Things quieten-down when I put the injector on as we emerge into open air and pass the Down Yard. There's a single-yellow ahead and I note that we're routed for the Down Local line through Raynes Park.

We cautiously cross over and Harold opens her up again such that we're back to 60 mph by Berrylands and things are eased as we touch 65 mph before Surbiton. Traffic is getting busier now as drowsy suburbanites emerge from their countless homes to converge upon Up platforms. Some stare at us in disbelief; some grin with delight... while the rest just ignore a 9F pounding along on, predominantly, electric trackage. Alternatively, those waiting upon Down Local platforms, step back in alarm as we busily pound through. This trip is indeed a doddle - a wonderful experience and the stuff dreams are made of!

Through Esher and onto Weybridge we rattle; (I've never known a Standard cab not to rattle from loose nuts and bolts, our 9F being no exception!). We pass the Addlestone Curve where, a few hours earlier and, seemingly in another world, we had diverged from the main line to toil up the grade to Staines! We're booked to stop at Woking for parcel and newspaper processing, so 65mph seems a nice pace to maintain as we commence an ever-steepening climb past Brooklands – home of British racing and the BAC.

Harold has reduced the cut-off to 15% in order to reduce the drafting but I'm still trying to keep her quiet! Closing the dampers-in has always been discouraged for its tendency to form clinker on the firebars much quicker than would normally be the case... but I do so anyway, even though this little lot has to proceed onwards to Southampton Terminus, it's downhill most of the way!

We pass a double-yellow followed by single-yellows in the distance and know for sure that the Woking Starter will be red - for commuter-traffic off the Pompey line. Harold shuts-off and lets her gradually lose momentum, such that we come to a leisurely stop at Woking. The crowds on the Up Side are thicker now, as the 06:00 hrs ex-Basing Semi Fast draws-in behind a U-Boat, and the few pundits on our platform, having watched that, are dodging porters and barrows to gain a close-up study of our unusual steed.

Enquiries are directed at us with tricky questions asked; one smart Alec asked if we knew how many spokes our driving wheels have! Without the slightest hesitation, Harold replies, "About a hundred and fifty, plus or minus a few we 'threw' on the way down!" There is a realisation of mockery and the smart Alec quickly retreats into the background.

The delightful 11 ½ mile long branch from Paddock wood to here at Hawkhurst was a great favourite for enthusiasts, but it seems not enough passengers to keep it open after 12 June 1961, even though there was a proposal at one point to electrify it. This view was taken three days before closure with H Class, 31177 from 73J Tonbridge on duty. *Dave Cobbe Collection/Rail Photoprints*

With van processing completed and all doors shut, the porters retire to their room for a well-earned cuppa... while we sit... and sit... before a red aspect. I curiously ask Harold, "How did you know about the number of spokes?" He replies that he didn't exactly, but knew that 5' – 0" wheels generally have about fifteen spokes each, so it was a matter of quick calculation towards an answer - totally unexpected by the questioner. I told him that it reminded me of a few years earlier - a South-Eastern driver reciting the same thing in the Bricklayers Arms lobby, while I was on loan to that shed as a passed cleaner. His charge was a Schools at London Bridge and his answer had been, "Enough to keep her off the ground, Sunshine!"

Our guard sidles up and anxiously enquires about the steam heating he'd requested. His jaw drops as I give him the bad news, followed by a definite redness to his temple and cheeks until I'm convinced that his head will explode at any second! But, no, there's an about-turn in best military fashion accompanied by a string of derisive mutterings concerning the 'diagramming' idiots at HQ!

As we sit there, it occurs to me that this was once Woking Common - the first extremity from Nine Elms Terminus of the old London & Southampton Railway. No doubt it was rural meadows on either side in those days! Harold gives a pop on the whistle – we've got the road, so I look rearward for the guard's tip; "Right away!" I call; the steam brake is released and the regulator nudged open. To a roar of open cylinder cocks, we nod cheerio to our audience and exit Woking Station to begin the last non-stop leg of our journey home. Being a doddle of a turn, there hasn't been much work for me to do other than a few shovelsful strategically spread to keep the grate covered with fuel. Over the Pompey junction we accelerate to 'tackle' the rest of the steepening climb through Brookwood to Milepost 31 just beyond Pirbright Junction.

With 25% cut-off and half regulator, we're up to 50 mph as we climb through the cutting at St John's, still on the Down Local line. I take occasional glances back along the train, not just to see how our vehicles are running but to keep a lookout for any fast traffic sneaking up on us on the Down Fast. Bulleid Pacifics, in particular, have a nasty habit of creating a vacuum around their torso at speed, and sucking flames from an open firehole door and unsuspecting crews'caps from their heads, while travelling in the same direction on an adjacent track!

As we approach Brookwood, I play a little imaginary tune on the whistle - to warn any unsuspecting passengers to stand clear. We whoosh through at 60 mph and, with the echoes from our machine still ringing in my ears, I start to make up a thicker fire with the intention to keep it that way so that my Eastleigh relief has something substantial to play with up through Worting to the top of the climb at Roundwood tunnel.

Suspecting that we must be the only train on the Down Local between Woking and Basing' at this hour of the morning, we anticipate a clear road right through. Being still on 'early turn', we have a 00:45 hrs start tomorrow morning and the possibility of getting relieved and going home early after this turn is a welcome thought, so Harold nudges her up to 65 mph!

Having decided that we're now an 'Express Parcels', we race under the Farnham flyover then lean to the right hand curve past Milepost 31 and dive into the jaws of Deepcut, all seemingly at the same time! I've begun keeping the exhaust steam injector tuned to demand and, with

this happily singing away, I begin to fire more frequently, spreading each charge as before.

We dive under the restrictive Basingstoke Canal, then out into the open past Sturt Lane Junction. There's movement down there as a five-coach local trundles southward behind an ex-GW Manor – a class I'd become familiar with during our regular jaunts north to Reading, Didcot and Oxford. Into a left-hand curved cutting, thence commencing a right hand curve at the approach to Farnborough. I whistle again, imagining that we're the Down Papers flashing under the road bridge and roaring through the station! Harold throws me a quizzical glance and I respond with a mischievous grin! Even enginemen get to play trains occasionally!

Onto the famous 'Racetrack' now and, pounding our way towards Fleet, we're climbing a very gradual incline with the four tracks as straight as a die interrupted only a few times by obtuse elbows. We roll onto a high embankment and the undulating countryside drops away on both sides; lower and lower it drops, such that, from our higher elevation, we can see north and south for miles! As we approach Fleet the surrounding landscape climbs again to reveal ponds on both sides. Another long blow on the whistle - just to warn 'no-one' standing too close to the edge of the platform – I'm loving this!

Once past Fleet the level ground on both sides rises to a long cutting with pine woods on either side. There's been very little to do with regard to boiler management – the engine seemingly taking care of itself! Harold has maintained 20% cut-off with the regulator barely open, it's difficult to accept that there's a train behind us. Having built-up a good fire for my Eastleigh relief, I fill the bucket with hot water from the injector pet-pipe. Back in my seat, I yawn and rub sore eyes from the night's activities.

Suddenly, I'm startled by thumping rail joints behind me followed by an increasingly loud hiss. Flames pour from the open firehole and my hat almost flies off my head as an express overtakes us on the Down Fast. Two Nine Elms' mischievous faces, aboard a Merchant Navy with only nine on, shoot past doing about 80 mph... I bet those Cockney hooligans enjoyed that!

"Gonna race 'em?" I shout in Harold's ear. "Not this time," he replies, "We're fifteen early as it is and might have to wait at the Basing' 'home' for a 'Reading' to cross over in front of us." I accept this logic and the fact that I'd rather finish this turn in a sedate fashion than a disappointing one!

Both trains roar through Winchfield, the last coach of the express drawing ahead of us. Hook is only a few miles away so, having restored my composure, I throw out the stewed remains of tea from my can then use the contents of the bucket to rinse away any grouts. I then procure soap and towel from my bag and tentatively wash-up in scalding water!

At last we thunder through Hook; it's been a long night, not in time but in events and this last stretch from Farnborough is always tedious and drawn-out. The long wooded cutting gradually gives way to a high embankment as we approach Old Basing village. I live down there and, as we cross the Basingstoke Canal this time, I play another tune on the whistle - to let mother know I'll be home soon.

Harold shuts off as the last Intermediate gantry comes into view - and she immediately lifts her safety valves. I become a little pensive – being so early, we might indeed clash withsomething off the Reading line and be held outside Basingstoke until he's clear. Our progress is slowing as the Outer Home comes into sight – it's off but its Distant is on. The East End Bobby obviously wants us to crawl our way towards the Home Signal, which is a bad sign, destroying all our hopes of an early book-off and, avoiding an encounter with our running foreman, and escape home!

We're down to an echoing clonk-clonk as we pass the East End Carriage Sidings. I feel quite sickly when I notice that the Home Signal is 'on' with the Down Local platform empty. This can only mean that something will cross our path and occupy it for as long as he takes.

Harold gives a little brake application and we come to a stand at the Home, safety valves roaring their heads off – will this engine ever keep quiet?! He looks over at me with a helpless expression and I shrug in response. Out comes his soap and towel and he washes-up while we wait for 'whatever'. But suddenly we hear a whirring sound, (Basingstoke gained electric semaphores three months previous, replacing the old pneumatic ones), and the Home is 'off'... "There's a Heaven after all," I rejoice, as Harold dries his hands and I tip the murky contents of the bucket over the side!

We give a toot on the whistle and accelerate quickly - just in case the bobby changes his mind! Perhaps the Down Local Platform was occupied by something that has recently drawn clear. Into our platform we trundle and notice two grinning reliefs rise from a bench and meander towards the water crane at the far end of the platform. We draw on... and on... up the platform to stop just right for water... much to the chagrin of the porters heaving their trolleys to keep up with us!

My relief hands his bag to his driver then hops up onto the tender while I step off the engine and swing the crane around for him to drop the pipe in. I open the valve just enough to provide a flow then hop back onto the footplate to collect my gear. The Eastleigh driver has already embarked and, still grinning broadly, announces to Harold that he had these beauties several times on the Fawley Oil turns and it was a wonder that Feltham surrendered it instead of the usual worn-out wrecks most sheds want rid-of!

After an experience to savour for a long time, we alight from our engine, bid our colleagues farewell and make our way cautiously across the running lines to the shed... And home for a good-day's sleep!

Thanks, Feltham!

Roger Carrell - West Australia 2017

Opposite: The Southern Railway anticipated a large volume of traffic to their new extension of the branch to Allhallows on Sea when it opened in 1932. Sadly the traffic did not materialise and the area around the location remained desolate, as a result the branch closed in 1961. On 24 September, 1960 the terminus welcomed H Class, 31512 with a special along the branch from Gravesend. *Colour Rail*

Branches & Byways

On 25 July, 1960 the Kent coalfield was very much active as Class O1, 31065 stands in the yard at Shepherds Well in between turns from here to the nearby Tilmanstone Colliery. This relic from Ashford Works in 1896 would be the last of her class in service, and as a result went for preservation, whilst of the fifty-five of her class that were inherited by British Railways in 1948, within two years this was whittled down to just eight examples. These 0-6-0s were designed by Stirling and introduced in 1878 for the South Eastern Railway. From 1903 until the last was dealt with in 1927 they were rebuilt as here by Wainwright for the South Eastern & Chatham Railway. Harry Wainwright went on to design the much loved H Class, with 31551 seen here at Oxted on 11 May, 1963 on a push-pull working. All save two of the sixty-six locomotives built entered service with the nationalised railway in 1948. Forty-five of these were converted to push-pull operation between 1949 and 1960.
Dave Cobbe Collection/Rail Photoprints & Colour Rail

As the pre-grouping locomotives disappeared from the area it would be Bulleid Class Q1s that would be sent out on local goods workings, as here with 33015 near Ockley with the 11:35 Dorking North to Horsham trip in November, 1963.
Strathwood Library Collection

Other classes of 0-6-0 would also be seen hereabouts as we find a combination of Class C2X 32526 and Q Class heading tender first through Baynards as light engines on 5 May, 1957. The passenger services along this charming line would cease on 14 June, 1965.

Strathwood Library Collection

All looked well at Bramley & Wonersh on 26 September the year beforehand, with 70C Guildford sending out Class Q1, 33012 for duty. There were a number of the stations on this line that were adjacent to level crossings, no doubt adding to their running costs for the accountants, intent on finding excuses to justify closures. *Colour Rail*

Not the usual angle for a view of the otherwise picturesque station at Rowfant on 9 June, 1963 showing the gated road crossing and the goods yard which was occupied by a substantial oil depot. The multi-tasking crossing keeper/porter is in position to accept the train staff from the driver of Class M7, 30053 heading for East Grinstead. Whereas the signalman at Hailsham collects the staff from the crew of N Class, 31871 off the line from Eridge with one of the British Railway's conversions of Maunsell stock into a two car push-pull set in tow. *Colour Rail*

A next to Ash near the large army camp at Aldershot. A number of routes once existed in this area including the closed loop via Ash Green Halt and Tongham which closed to passengers in 1937. However this section of the line from Ascot to Guildford was electrified, but also carried services off the non-electrified route from Reading to Guildford, as witnessed by Standard Class 4MT Mogul, 76060 from 71A Eastleigh on 24 January, 1959. *Colour Rail*

The curve from the Waterloo to Reading line here at Virginia Water would normally be served by a regular EMU service to link up with the LSWR mainline at Weybridge. It would also enjoy a large number of freights each day and the odd empty stock working as here with one of the short framed Class M7s, fitted with round splashers and sand boxes under the running plate. When there were accidents or engineering works on the West of England mainline between Weybridge and Clapham Junction this route would become a lifeline for all the diverted traffic. *Colour Rail*

Opposite and above: Towards the end of Southern Region steam if you wanted to enjoy steam locomotives on branch lines the choices were slim with just the line from Lymington Pier back to Brockenhurst, or ironically here in the heart of London at Kensington Olympia. On 19 May, 1966 the ecs is departing back to Clapham Junction behind Standard Class 4MT, 80143 after the morning rush hour. All three designs of Standard tank locomotives found employment on the region, including examples of the thirty strong 2MT 2-6-2Ts. Among the short term replacements for the Adams Radial Tanks on the Axminster to Lyme Regis branch was 84022 in 1961 supplied by 72A Exmouth Junction. *Strathwood Library Collection & Colour Rail*

Three of these Adams Radial Tanks were retained for the branch from here at Axminster along the tight curvature of the branch to Lyme Regis. On 8 August, 1959 we see 30584 setting back into the bay at Axminster with through coaches off the West of England Mainline, with holiday makers for Lyme Regis.
Dave Cobbe/Collection Rail Photoprints

Its Ivatt 2MT, 41291 charged with keeping the stock warm for today's LCGB East Devon (No.2) rail tour which had classmate 41206 sharing the duties along the branch from here at Axminster to Lyme Regis, as they await the arrival of their passengers on 7 March, 1965. *Dave Cobbe Collection/Rail Photoprints*

Soon to depart off the Somerset & Dorset line for a spell at Hereford before returning to Southern metals at Exmouth Junction, was Standard Class 3MT, 82002. Here it passes the shed at Templecombe coded 71H by the Southern Region, and variously 82G and 83G by the Western Region. On 4 August, 1962 this local from Bournemouth West was in the hands of 82002, whilst it was still allocated here as 82G.
Dave Cobbe Collection/Rail Photoprints

Another Western Region interloper complete with their stock at Yeovil Town on 23 March 1963, was one of the Collett designed Pannier Tanks fitted for push-pull operation. Freshly allocated to here at 72C Yeovil Town the month beforehand it would find employment on "The Bunk" as the locals called it between Yeovil's Junction and Town stations. The reign of this locomotive would be short, ending that August, previously it had been the preserve of Class M7s. *Strathwood Library Collection*

Opposite: One of the longer term residents here at Yeovil for the shuttle services between Yeovil's three stations, Town, Junction and Pen Mill was Class M7, 30131. It came from Bournemouth shed in September 1951, and remained here until withdrawn in December, 1962. It was in action on 15 August, 1959 being driven from the front of this ex LSWR gate stock push-pull set, heading for Yeovil Junction and away from the Town station. *Dave Cobbe Rail Photoprints*

Right: Things look very cold today for another of the push-pull fitted Class M7s, this time it's the much transferred 30052 in the harsh winter of 1963, as it tries to keep its push-pull set warm. Between 1948 and its withdrawal in May 1964, this M7 found itself re-allocated fourteen times. A light intermediate overhaul at Eastleigh Works in the early autumn of 1962, saw it fitted with AWS. *Colour Rail*

Another Western Region invader intent on deposing Drummond Class M7s from their stomping grounds was this Collett designed 0-4-2T, on another cold day this time on 1 February 1965 at Seaton. It had first been based at Yeovil with its push-pull ability in use there, it has now found its way to this ex LSWR branch from Seaton Junction as a result of the branch being transferred to the control of the Western Region since 1 January, 1963. The Western Region would also seek to draft in its own locomotives in order to replace the venerable Beattie Well Tanks on the Wenford Bridge branch with their own Collett 0-6-0PTs from the 1366 Class after 1962. Onlookers young and old watch the flagman protect the passage of 30587 on this un-gated crossing near Dunmere. Thankfully both this locomotive and 1442 evaded the scrap men and have survived in preservation. *Both: Colour Rail*

On 1 July, 1964 this leg of the Atlantic Coast Express from Waterloo has arrived at Wadebridge today behind 34078 222 Squadron, sadly this Exmouth Junction allocated Battle of Britain Pacific would soon be withdrawn in two months time. Local stopping services here at Wadebridge were still in the hands of Drummond's Class T9s such as 30709 on 28 April, 1959. One of the Beattie Well Tanks shunts the station yard in between jaunts on the Wenford Bridge branch. *Dave Cobbe/Rail Photoprints & Colour Rail*

Opposite: The headcode of 34066 Spitfire, suggests this as a Waterloo - Plymouth service as the Bulleid Pacific tackles Honiton bank. This was the same locomotive involved in the dreadful collision in the fog at Lewisham on the early evening of 4 December, 1957 that claimed ninety lives and saw one hundred and seventy-three injured. *Colour Rail*

Right: There is steam to spare onboard an unkempt 34030 Watersmeet from Exmouth Junction near Launceston in August, 1964. The headcode denotes a passenger service on the Exeter Central to Padstow stretch of the former LSWR. This would be another of the Bulleid Light Pacifics to face withdrawal in September 1964 at the close of that summer's timetable. *Colour Rail*

Opposite: Station staff are braving the April shower of rain as Ivatt 2MT, 41317 draws into Bere Alston on 29 April, 1963 in expectation of parcels traffic or heavy luggage. *Colour Rail*

Above: The Class M7s such as 30024 leaving Sidmouth Junction for Exmouth on 31 July, 1960 would soon be displaced by Ivatt 2MTs and Standard Class 3MT & 4MT tanks. *Dave Cobbe Collection/Rail Photoprints*

Right: Whereas it would be Pannier Tanks that would depose the Adams Class O2s soon after this view of 30199 at Wadebridge with a Bodmin North train in September, 1959. *Colour Rail*

This Standard Class 3MT, had arrived at 72A Exmouth Junction when new in September 1952, so it was no stranger really at Sidmouth in 1959. Always a Southern Region locomotive, 82019 would next find work out of Eastleigh briefly in 1962, before settling in at 70A Nine Elms until the end of steam in July, 1967. Staff are on hand to supervise cars being loaded and unloaded at Okehampton on 29 August, 1964 just as Maunsell N Class, 31845 draws in. *Both: Colour Rail*

A busy moment is recorded at Torrington on 10 June, 1964 as a passenger service gets away, leaving Ivatt 2MT 41248 to set off with a very short goods train. It would all draw to a close here at Torrington in 1965. We take our leave of the West Country at Exeter Central in May 1964 as 34061 73 Squadron starts away with an up stopper for Salisbury. *Both: Colour Rail*

Bournemouth's Belle

The driver of 35008 Orient Line watches out in expectation of a clear run on one of the region's most prestigious services as the down Bournemouth Belle gracefully sweeps through Weybridge, whilst an EPB service back to Waterloo via Virginia Water awaits departure in the background during 1962. Cleanliness standards also had slipped badly for our next view of this service in July, 1964 as 35005 Canadian Pacific runs past the long since redundant central platforms at Farnborough. *Strathwood Library Collection & Colour Rail*

This is how it should be as 34017 Ilfracombe hurries through Raynes Park in December, 1961. Or perhaps when the headboard was still carried as here by 34064 Fighter Command ready for departure time at Bournemouth West and a fast run to Waterloo on 26 April, 1955. *Colour Rail*

Left: The impressive signal box at the north end of Eastleigh station has set the road for the safe and unhindered passage of the Bournemouth Belle on this day headed by 35018 British India Line still in her original guise as Oliver Vaughan Snell Bulleid CBE had envisaged for his Pacifics. Two years later and this would be the first of her class to be rebuilt and released to traffic once more on 14 February, 1956. *Colour Rail*

Opposite: Several versions of this blue livery were tried on a number of the Merchant Navy Pacifics in the early 1950s, this is 35012 United States Lines ready for departure at Waterloo in June, 1951. *Colour Rail*

Right: Several admirers take a moment on the platforms at Clapham Junction to enjoy the passing of the Pullman stock of this morning's down Bournemouth Belle in 1964. Pullman cars were added to a number of Bournemouth services originally by the LSWR, but it was after the grouping that the Southern Railway created what would be known as the Bournemouth Belle as a daily service in 1936. At the outbreak of World War Two the service was suspended, motive power up until then had usually been a Lord Nelson. On 7 October, 1946 and now rostered for Merchant Navy haulage the service begun once more, with stops at Southampton Central and Bournemouth Central.
Strathwood Library Collection

Its May 1956 and the first two of the rebuilt Merchant Navy Pacifics are posed for this shot at Southampton Central, as both 35018 British India Line and 35020 Bibby Line make an impressive sight, even though the British Railways Board's Modernisation Plan published a year beforehand suggests lots of changes to come! One of the main problems for the railway in many parts of the country, was recruitment. Low pay compared to industry and commerce, and starting off as a cleaner on perhaps the likes of 35008 Orient Line, seen brewing up nicely before departing Waterloo in June 1966.

Colour Rail & Ian Turnbull/Rail Photoprints

Left and below: All was as it should be back in August of 1959, when 35017 Belgian Marine was recorded at the same spot. The Belle was set to depart from Bournemouth West in the up direction at 16:35, on this occasion hauled by 35015 Rotterdam Lloyd resplendent in blue still in 1951. A two minute stop was made at Bournemouth Central, departing at 16:45. From here to Southampton Central a time of thirty three minutes was allowed, before setting of with the fastest start to stop timing of the day from Southampton Central to Waterloo of eighty-five minutes for the journey of 79.2 miles. *Colour Rail*

Opposite: The Pullman Brakes would unfortunately be replaced in the last days of this wonderful named train by Mark I Full Brakes, initially plain maroon liveried examples, which were later exchanged for chocolate & cream ones from the Western Region. This was all still to come when 35030 Elder Dempster Lines set off after the customary stop here at Southampton Central in August, 1964 although the name boards have already been dropped. *Both: Colour Rail*

Left: One last look back at this much loved service departing Southampton Central for Bournemouth in 1954 behind 35014 Nederland Line in lined green, it was an example that adopted this livery from malachite green three years earlier, and missed out on blue completely. *Colour Rail*

Opposite: Having brought an express into Brighton in August 1959, the crew onboard 30795 Sir Dinadan may be a relief who are now booked to take the Maunsell Class N15, off to the adjacent engine shed for disposal. *Colour Rail*

Around the Links

Time to relax for the crew of this scruffy looking Class M7, as they wait at Brockenhurst in August, 1963. Whilst they are not keen enough to put some shine back to their engine, at least the station staff can have pride in their station gardens that summer with a nice display of colour for passengers and themselves. The smartened up appearance of Class D, 31737 from 74D Tonbridge shed is worthy of a shot as it comes off the RCTS Invicta Railtour at Rainham on 12 September, 1954. It will be replaced by Class R, 31671 lurking behind it for the next leg of the tour. *Both: Colour Rail*

The cleaners have missed the front end of Black 5, 44917 from 71G Bath Green Park at the other end of the Somerset & Dorset line from here at Bournemouth West on 25 May, 1956.
Strathwood Library Collection

The effects of regular cleaning of the smoke deflectors of 34100 Appledore, once a regular on the Golden Arrow have left their mark on the paintwork. Whilst the crew of 34066 Spitfire with its battered side casing look on at the approaches to Weymouth shed in 1966.
Denis Feltham

There would never be much glamour for Feltham's four Urie Class G16s, they would from time to time be let off hump shunting in the yard to stretch their legs on goods workings to the likes of the yards at Willesden as here around 1960. Another longer term resident of 70B Feltham was 33009, today found pottering around light engine at Clapham Junction, nothing too taxing. *Both: Colour Rail*

Both the Wainwright L Class, 31776 and its Maunsell coaches let the side down for passengers at Tunbridge Wells West towards the close of the 1950s. Two young lads are on hand at Salisbury to note the appearance of 30829, one of Maunsell's Class S15s in their books in 1963. Although it was most likely a real common sight to them as it spent all of its British Railways life shedded here. *Colour Rail & Strathwood Library Collection*

We have already heard what it was like to have a run in a Class 9F to here at Basingstoke in our introduction from one of the depot's ex-fireman Roger Carrell. In October 1965 the driver of 2A Tyseley allocated 92212 heads for the shed having worked a freight into the area. A contrast in size to the mighty 2-10-0 would be Adams Class B4, 30102 in between shunts at Winchester City during 1963. Whilst this small but powerful 0-4-0T would soon be withdrawn that September and 92212 would work on into 1968, both would find their way into the preservation movement. The 9F via Woodhams Scrapyard at Barry, and the B4 via Sir Billy Butlin and his holiday camp at Ayr in Scotland upon withdrawal.

Strathwood Library Collection & Rail Photoprints

Opposite: A look back to see all is well at Eastleigh on 6 April 1966, as 44942 from 2D Banbury heads back in the direction of home complete with someone's political affinities declared on its tender. *Colour Rail*

Right: Someone else has perhaps made a start on cleaning up around the bunker of 30321, one of the shorter wheelbase Class M7s at Clapham Junction in August 1959. *Gerald T. Robinson*

Below: No such care for this push-pull fitted H Class at Oxted on 27 March, 1961. *Strathwood Library Collection*

There was still a fair degree of pride in the job for maintaining the appearance of this elderly Class T9 at Brockenhurst back in the 1950s. Starting its British Railways career in Devon, based at Plymouth's ex LSWR shed at Friary, it would soon head for Wiltshire and spend the next twenty-one months allocated to 72B Salisbury, before her last move to 71A Eastleigh. Until the decision to list her as withdrawn in November, 1959. Bringing an end to a sixty year working life for this product of the LSWR's works at Nine Elms. An even earlier offspring from this south London works was Class M7, 30249 which emerged in May, 1897. When seen bringing empty stock into Clapham Junction in October, 1958 this fellow Drummond locomotive would manage almost five more years of service to the railway. *Strathwood Library Collection & Dave Cobbe Collection/Rail Photoprints*

Bulleid's fitting of a Lemaitre Exhaust and larger chimney is working well on Maunsell's Schools Class 30938 St. Olave's as she climbs Grosvenor Bank out of Victoria in June, 1959 with the 09:26 service to Ramsgate and the Kent Coast. Further along the South Coast to another sea side resort at Bournemouth to find Class M7, 30036 engaged in a little shunting activity. Signs of foreboding are at hand as a Drewry built diesel shunter can be seen alongside. *Colour Rail*

The short wheelbase USA tanks had been brought to Southampton's sometimes tightly curved track work around the streets and within the docks after World War Two as they offered an inexpensive way of modernising the fleet here, and a chance to dispose of some of the pre-grouping locomotives on such duties. However the replacements for USA tanks such as 30069 at work amongst Southampton's road traffic on 26 April, 1962, were not far away. Deliveries of the fourteen Ruston & Hornsby diesel shunters to take over this work would all be delivered in the next seven months. The DMU replacements for the Sidmouth branch have already displaced steam and stands in the bay at Sidmouth Junction in April, 1964. A filthy 35013 Blue Funnel has today's Atlantic Coast Express as footplate staff go about their business at Sidmouth Junction. *Colour Rail & Dave Cobbe Collection/Rail Photoprints*

Opposite: We should perhaps be thankful that someone has taken the trouble to clean the cabside of Standard Class 4MT Mogul, 76068 drawing stock out of the sidings at Fratton on 14 August, 1965. This Doncaster built locomotive was barely nine years old, and although being allocated to 71A Eastleigh from new, it was weeks from being listed as withdrawn in October 1965. *Strathwood Library Collection*

Doncaster and Derby Works also built small numbers of the tank engine version of the Standard Class 4MT, although the bulk of the class including 80137 would be built at the former LBSCR works at Brighton. This example at Waterloo on ecs work, was among those exchanged with the London Midland Region for Brighton built Fairburn Class 4MTs in late 1959. *Len Smith*

The AWS boxes under the smokeboxes of both of these Merchant Navy Pacifics stand out well here, as do the electric headcode lamps on both 35008 Orient Line in 1965 at Southampton Central, and on 35029 Ellerman Lines, which has just backed onto its train Waterloo in 1963. *Strathwood Library Collection*

Certainly the driver of Standard 4MT Mogul, 76060 is giving his charge some stick as they bark away from Basingstoke around 1960, with what looks like a pretty heavy inter-regional service. Whereas classmate 76039 is not one of the Southern Region's native locomotives, having arrived here in the carriage sidings at Clapham Junction on 16 April, 1965 from 1A Willesden most likely on an inter-regional freight working via Kensington Olympia. *Both: Strathwood Library Collection*

Ex Works Eastleigh

34051

34051

The alterations to some of the tenders attached to Bulleid's light pacifics resulted in two distinct style of livery for the un-rebuilt members in the later British Railways era. Which we can compare here between 34051 Winston Churchill in the autumn of 1963, and 34054 Lord Beaverbrook in June 1961, both at the same spot outside the works at Eastleigh. *Both: Colour Rail*

When Feltham's Class H16s went to Eastleigh for works attention in previous years they had been sent back to return the their regular duties in south-west London after any work. However in January, 1960 two of the five locomotives in the class found themselves re-allocated to 71A Eastleigh. So it was, that 30516 would remain in the area after repairs and take up duties on local freights, then the following year the remaining three of the class joined them here at Eastleigh for a short time also, before all of them returned to their spiritual home at Feltham once more until withdrawn late in 1962. Brighton Works had built this Fairburn Class 4MT, for duties on the Southern in 1951, but shortly after this view was taken at Eastleigh in 1959, 42082 would be one of those swapped with the London Midland Region in exchange for Standard Class 4MTs, in an attempt to focus spares and knowledge of classes. This example going to 14D Neasden for its next duties on ex Great Central routes. *Colour Rail & Strathwood Library Collection*

The USA tanks were common enough around Eastleigh, but the sight of an ex-works 30066 caught our cameraman's attention during a society visit to the shed in April 1960. This engine was withdrawn from regular traffic in December 1962, and took up the identity of DS235 in March 1963 to replace the Terriers that had been acting as works shunters at Lancing Carriage Works. She was joined by classmate 30074 which became DS236, both would be withdrawn in August 1965. After Brighton Works had ceased overhauling locomotives in 1958, the responsibility of looking after the ex LBSCR engines started to fall upon Eastleigh more and more as repairs at Ashford were being run down, therefore the appearance of Billington's K Class, 32339 in 1962 might have been regarded by spotters in the area as a treat. Indeed it was as all of the class were rendered extinct in November and December 1962. *Both: Strathwood Library Collection*

On shed at Eastleigh on 9 May, 1959 was 34079 141 Squadron which had just completed a general overhaul, including the cutting down of the tender raves. At this time she was based out of 72A Exmouth Junction having previously been on the eastern section at 74B Ramsgate. *Colour Rail*

Taking in the sunshine at Eastleigh's shed on 24 September, 1955 was one of the Urie designed King Arthurs, 30750 Morgan Le Fay. She had just completed a general overhaul and would be withdrawn less than two years later, with 1,298,672 miles credited to her record card. *Colour Rail*

Another good long term servant to the railway, was this Drummond 700 Class or Black Motor. This recent overhaul of 30699 in 1954, might have to see it through for its last seven years out of its sixty-four year career. In May 1956 it was the turn of 35013 Blue Funnel to be paraded out as the latest rebuilt Merchant Navy alongside the works offices from where this lovely elevated view was taken. She would record 1,114, 658 miles upon withdrawal at the close of Southern Region steam in 1967, just over half of these after this rebuild. *Both: Colour Rail*

Fireman are at work trimming their coal at Eastleigh's shed in June 1951, as we focus upon 34007 Wadebrdge which has recently undergone its first general overhaul after just over five years of traffic. Her cab has been modified to the more familiar wedge shape, but she still carries the flares around the buffer beam in front of the cylinders. She had also lost the original malachite livery in favour of the now accepted British Railways lined green. By the autumn of 1958, Eastleigh Works were well accomplished at rebuilding Bulleid Pacifics, as 34031 Torrington was only in works for forty-nine days before appearing outside for us to admire. *Both: Colour Rail*

Although we have already seen 35018 British India Line at Southampton Central, we couldn't resist this shot of her freshly rebuilt in February, 1956 and in the familiar spot outside the works in full view of the mainline to show off their craftsmanship. Construction of Bulleid's Q1 0-6-0 design was shared between Brighton and Ashford Works during 1942. This one was from the former SECR works in Kent, and in April 1963 had just completed what would be her last heavy intermediate overhaul, being witdrawn as a 70A Nine Elms locomotive in January 1966 as one of the last three in use.

Colour Rail & Strathwood Library Collection

The preparation crew of N Class, 31408 look like they are getting some pretty solid fuel for the next turn out of 70C Guildford on 8 March, 1966. The same cannot be said for what is in the tender of Ivatt Class 2MT, 46509 here at 70A Nine Elms from 1A Willesden to work a special on 27 May, 1965. *Colour Rail & Strathwood Library Collection*

The coal is nicely trimmed onboard 30923 Bradfield at her home shed 73B Bricklayers Arms on 31 August 1961, as today's fireman is sure she has a full tender. The tender of 30854 Howard of Effingham looks like it is in need of a generous refill from Eastleigh's coal stage. There is no trace of this same locomotive's damage from a rollover down the bank at Shawford in the summer of 1952. *Strathwood Library Collection & Colour Rail*

A study of front ends of two sister Maunsell Class S15s at Eastleigh on 26 July 1963 as our conscientious driver oils around the motion of his steed for today's turn. It looks like another of Maunsell's designs, his 0-6-0 Q Class is just being brought back into steam for the first time after a minor works visit next door at Eastleigh. Maunsell's successor Bulleid was at the helm when the twenty locomotives of this class were constructed. They were built with single chimneys originally, but as poor steamers it was decided by Bulleid to cure this by fitting them with multiple jet blast pipes and a larger diameter chimney. Due to corrosion, some would later be fitted with spare single chimneys from British Railways Standards. *Both: Colour Rail*

One wonders just how dry the fireman would remain onboard 30800 Sir Meleaus de Lile performing firing duties out on the road, judging from the stormy looking sky in the background to this view from September, 1956 at 73F Ashford. The footplate of 34071 601 Squadron appears far more weather proof outside the running sheds at 71A Eastleigh, as a more senior colleague gives clear instruction to his junior. *Both: Colour Rail*

Overalls would not stay clean for long working in this kind of environment, no matter what you washed them with. The shed yard at Gillingham in June 1959, the shed's code changed this month from 73D to 73J. *Colour Rail*

The view from the balconies of the nearby flats overlooking the turntable at 70A Nine Elms, afforded a great view of 80143 clattering off the turntable in May, 1967, within two months these disturbances to the residents would be a thing of the past. *George Woods*

Another turntable view this time of the much shallower pit that formed access to the shed roads at 70C Guildford. In July 1964, this was the home shed for 33015 one of the Brighton built examples of Bulleid's Q1s. Her last general overhaul at Eastleigh had been nearly two years ago, had she seen the attentions of any cleaners since? This run down condition is echoed by K Class, 32347 at Three Bridges on 5 May, 1961 also on its home shed. *Late Norman Browne/Strathwood Library Collection & Gerald T. Robinson*

It was not usual to find any cleaners left at Nine Elms by 13 August, 1966. However, the arrival Peppercorn Pacific 60532 Blue Peter from its Scottish base for a rail tour was reason enough to get out the paintbrush to smarten her up once again. The presence of the preserved Drummond T9, on the LCGB organised Sussex Coast Limited has aroused lots of local interest here at Guildford on 13 August, 1962.
Colour Rail & Strathwood Library Collection

Going well with seven coaches, one more than officially allowed over the Alps near Alton on 9 January, 1966 was this first running of the LCGB's S15 Commemorative Railtour, not a bad show considering this locomotive had been out of service for over five months at this time. On 2 December 1962 another over subscribed last run was made with 30585 & 30587 as the South Western Suburban Railtour. This is the duo at Surbiton on their way to meet Class H16 30517 after a trip down the Hampton Court branch. The second tour ran on 16 December, 1962 and all three of the Beattie Well Tanks were then duly withdrawn as was 30517. *Colour Rail & Tony Butcher*

The RCTS arranged two tours to visit the Longmoor Miltary Railway during April 1966, this is the second tour on the 30th of the month. This pairing of Maunsell Moguls had started the tour from Waterloo that morning and were now put back on for the early evening jaunt back from here at Windsor & Eton Riverside the twenty-seven miles back to Waterloo, which they did in seventy four minutes. *Strathwood Library Collection*

The motive power for the REC's South Western Adams Radial Tank Railtour on 19 March, 1961 would be 30582. This Class 0415 tank had been prepared that morning at 70A Nine Elms for the 13:58 departure from Waterloo. From here at Staines the lightly loaded three coach special would head for Windsor & Eton with a full compliment of passengers. Originally there had been seventy-one of these 4-4-2Ts to work the LSWR's suburban services before the electrification rendered all but three of them extinct. At the time of this tour 30584 had just been withdrawn, leaving this tour locomotive and 30583 to soldier on until that July, when they too were withdrawn, however 30583 found sanctuary on the Bluebell Railway, thankfully. *Colour Rail*

On 10 March 1963, the restored Class T9, 120 had brought the Southern Counties Touring Society's *Hampshire Venturer* from Waterloo to here at Andover Junction, where Class Q1, 33039 was provided to take the train to Bulford Camp via Grateley and return. Then the T9 would take them to Southampton where USA tank, 30074 would give them a run along the branch to Fawley. Another tour to Fawley involving a pair of USA tanks this time was run on 20 March 1966, with 30073 & 30064 running back to back, note the differing bunkers of the pair.

C H Gooch railwayimages.com & Strathwood Library Collection

The preserved Class T9, 120 saw action once again on three legs of the LCGB's Sussex Coast Limited tour on 24 June, 1962. Having doubleheaded with 120 from Eastbourne, Class M7, 30005 comes off at Rotherfield to leave 120 to carry on to London Bridge. More double heading again on 13 June, 1965 as this pairing of Maunsell Moguls 31803 & 31411 make a photostop at Heathfield on their way from Three Bridges towards Hastings. *Late Vincent Heckford/Strathwood Library Collection & Dave Southern*

Two famous locomotives being turned whilst on specials, 4472 Flying Scotsman needs no introduction and always draws admirers. As here at Basingstoke on 10 September, 1966 having brought the Gainsborough Model Railway Society's Farnborough Flyer to the area for an air show. Just about to make its last journey from here at Newhaven Harbour to Eastleigh and an all too swift scrapping process, was the very last Atlantic 4-4-2 wheel arrangement locomotive at work on British Railways 32424 Beachy Head, it has just worked the first leg of the RCTS Sussex Coast Limited on 13 April, 1958. *Tony Butcher & Colour Rail*

Doomed

A depressing sight in the yard at the now closed 70E Salisbury on 1 October 1967, where Standard Class 4MT, 80146 formerly allocated to Bournemouth heads a line-up of condemned locomotives. *Derek Jones*

On 22 October 1967 both 35012 United States Lines and 34044 Woolacombe await their entry into the scrap yard of John Cashmore at Newport, just over three months after the end of steam operations on the Southern Region. *Derek Jones*

The trail of withdrawn Bulleid Pacifics began in 1963, with ten light Pacifics sent to Eastleigh for scrapping. The following year 34065 Hurricane was among the next wave of casualties which was now including some of the rebuilds too. *Strathwood Library Collection*

Among the long line of withdrawn locomotives awaiting disposal at 70B Feltham by the entrance to the shed on 12 April, 1963 was Maunsell's W Class, 31923. It was just one of a large number of steam locomotives posted as withdrawn by the Southern Region towards the end of the previous year. There were more Maunsell casualties from this purge in 1962, all dumped near Hove station during the winter months. Among some of the Schools Class still here on 5 May, 1963 was 30911 Dover they were all awaiting their destiny with the scrapper's acetylene torches.
Jim Oatway & Mike Morant Collection

Many of the former LSWR's 4-4-0s had already perished to the cutters at Eastleigh Works, however by 18 September 1960 their numbers were starting to get a bit thinner still with Class T9 30288 and two classmates awaiting their turn. *Gerald T. Robinson*

Before long even relative youngsters such as Standard Class 2MT, 84014 would be deemed out of favour too. It was seen outside Eastleigh's running shed on 19 December, 1965 having been brought here for assessment to see if the class might be replacements for the ageing Adams Class O2s on the Isle of Wight. *Peter Coton*

Opposite: The chance to make use of the relatively new Standards was not taken. Instead a decision to electrify just a fraction of the routes on the Isle of Wight and purchase redundant 1927 built tube stock from London Transport, was deemed as the way forward. So it would be that 36 Carisbrooke and all the other remaining Class O2s on the island and stations such as Ashey, seen here on 23 June, 1963 would be lost. *Colour Rail*

Isle of Wight Memories

Yes perhaps it was all a working museum, but just think how much of a tourist attraction it would make today, not to mention helping relieve some of the road traffic for the island. Running round and about to enter the tunnel at Ventnor West on 4 September, 1965 was 31 Chale. Whilst another visit two years beforehand catches the crew of 18 Ningwood exchanging the token at the often busy, during the summer timetable at least, Smallbrook Junction. *Both: Tony Butcher*

The line from here at Ryde Pier Head as far as Shanklin would be retained and electrified. But on 31 August 1965 it was the likes of 29 Alverstone that would meet trippers off the ferry. Next stop off the pier was here at Ryde Esplanade where the arrival of 14 Fishbourne is being missed by a passenger more interested in shipping perhaps. Some idea of the varied nature of the ancient rolling stock can be gauged from this view.
Strathwood Library Collection

Newport was in its heyday as an important junction for the island, with four lines meeting here from Cowes, Freshwater, Ryde and two routes to Ventnor. In the summer of 1965, number 18 Ningwood is taking water at the station which looks busy just now. Not all of the coaching stock was to be seen running in a tatty condition, as witnessed here at Haven Street behind 30 Shorwell in June 1964. *Strathwood Library Collection & Colour Rail*

Although Haven Street seen overleaf would be saved as a preservation scheme, the closure of the branch from Brading to here at the charming terminus at Bembridge would see closure on 21 September, 1953. In July 1951 everything looked clean and tidy as 15 Cowes waits to depart. Whilst 15 Cowes was an earlier withdrawal in June 1956, 14 Fishbourne seen here approaching Smallbrook Junction in September 1963 with a goods for Cowes would remain until the end of steam in December, 1966. *Colour Rail & Tony Butcher*

The tall bracket signal near Ryde St. Johns allows early sighting to the crew of 33 Bembridge as it heads for Shanklin on 7 August, 1965. The line beyond Shanklin to Ventnor would close on 18 April, 1966. *Gerald T. Robinson*

Opposite: An RCTS tour of the island brought enthusiasts to Cowes on 18 May, 1952. As we are reminded that the Adams Class O2s did not hold a complete monopoly on the system. At this time there were four Class E1s all named, still at work. This is 3 Ryde which worked the legs from Newport to here at Cowes and back. *Colour Rail*

At Brading where the line to St. Helens and Bembridge had once diverted is our next stop in 1966, where we see 35 Freshwater passing the short home starter signal heading for Shanklin. *Strathwood Library Collection*

Opposite: One or two examples of the island's Class O2s were painted in unlined black for a short while, but they were much more attractive as here with 31 Chale, on shed at Newport on 18 May, 1952. When the shed codes were allocated in 1950, Newport became 71E which it retained until 30 September, 1954 when it adopted 70G until closure on 4 November, 1957. *Strathwood Library Collection*

The choice of locomotives that could work without any restrictions on the island was due to the dimensions within the tunnel at Ventnor. The four Class E1s were used on goods trains and for shunting at Medina Wharf, this is 4 Wroxall on shed at Newport in May 1949. This livery based around the Southern Railway livery would be discarded in favour of plain black within a few years. Whilst the Class O2s such as 32 Bonchurch seen here the same day at Newport would enjoy a lined black mixed traffic livery. *Colour Rail*

Not only was there the engine shed at Newport, but storage sidings for stock too. As the 1960s progressed the railway activity here shrank, until closure completely the year after this view of 26 Whitwell working the 13:30 Ryde to Cowes on 3 October, 1965. Ryde shed was coded 71F in 1950, later to become 70H as of 30 September, 1954. This along with the locomotive works across the other side of the station at Ryde St. Johns Road would become the main focus for enthusiasts. This was especially so on 31 December, 1966 as 27 Merstone has its needs attended to on the last day of public steam services. *Dave Southern & Tony Butcher*

Opposite: Working with steam locomotives is certainly a mucky job, and being on the Isle of Wight is no exception as this driver oils round on 16 Ventnor on 1 September, 1965. The alternative use for the wheelbarrow in both views is born out on 17 Seaview as her driver sets about the Westinghouse donkey pump in May the previous year at Ryde.
Late Dave Down & Colour Rail

Thankfully not all of the remaining fleet were left unkempt by cleaners, although one suspects not a lot has been afforded to cleaning below the footplate of 25 Godshill in this view. This was one of eleven of the class transferred to Ryde upon closure of Newport shed in the autumn of 1957.
Strathwood Library Collection

Another reminder of how things appeared in the earlier part of the 1960s with 26 Whitwell, looking a credit to Ryde shed in 1962. Towards the end of the following season however it is a very down at heel 35 Freshwater, that is seen getting away from Ryde St. Johns in September, 1963. During the winter timetable a number of the class would be set aside into storage, and it allowed Ryde Works to catch up on overhauls.
Strathwood Library Collection & Tony Butcher

Let it Snow, Let it Snow

Opposite: Making an impressive start from Ryde St. Johns with a Ventnor service on 25 August, 1964 was 33 Bembridge, the island's railway works can be seen to the right with a freshly overhauled coach awaiting entry back to traffic. *Rail Photoprints*

In Contrast to a lovely summer's day on the Isle of Wight, how about a freezing morning on the platform at Oxted? A morning when many trains would no doubt have been delayed, so the appearance of 34055 Fighter Pilot lifts our sprits. *Colour Rail*

Diligent staff have been at work clearing away snow from the platforms for the benefit of any passengers brave enough to venture out this morning here at Farnborough in January, 1963. Imagine what it must have been like that morning for the crew preparing 73083 Pendragon for this duty. *Colour Rail*

No doubt likewise for the crew of 34017 Ilfracombe, as they keep themselves out of the wind on the footplate as they hurry along at Marden, on the racing stretch between Tonbridge and Ashford. *Colour Rail*

In January 1954, heavy snow has fallen along the south coast as the crew of this Brighton to Bournemouth service push onwards from their stop at Southampton Central, behind 32421 South Foreland. This Marsh Atlantic would bow out of service in August 1956 allocated to 75A Brighton.

No doubt the sights and sounds from the exhaust of Ivatt Class 2MT, 41300 could be seen and heard for some distance across Run Common in January 1963, as the locomotive heads a Guildford to Horsham local. *Both: Colour Rail*

Left and opposite: Snow greets 35001 Channel Packet at Lymington Junction at the head of a down Bournemouth service still made up with blood & custard stock. On another cold day when only the brave would venture out with their camera to visit Bricklayers Arms to record C Class 31271 standing outside the long shed, whilst an engine crew set about turning a Standard Class 4MT in these inhospitable conditions. This 0-6-0 would be the last of her class to be cut up in December 1967, having adopted the departmental service number DS240 in July 1963 for work at Ashford. *Both: Colour Rail*

There is no shortage of luggage and parcels capacity at the front of this down train arriving at Southampton Central during January 1963, with 34089 602 Squadron at its helm. This Battle of Britain Pacific had been rebuilt in the autumn of 1960 after twelve years of service. *Colour Rail*

Two further scenes after the snowstorms during the winter of 1954, firstly on shed at Eastleigh as the rays of sunshine and the heat from nearby engines, start to thaw out this diminutive P Class, 31558 which had only lost its old Southern Railway number and livery two years previously. Then across to the station at Eastleigh in time to see the much more impressive one hundred and thirty-nine ton bulk of Urie's Class H15, 30487 drawing in on the down slow line. *Both: Colour Rail*

Snowy weather has never been a good playmate for the Southern's third rail EMU fleet and the harsh winter that struck in 1963 would be no exception. On 9 January we find one of the 4-SUBs tucked away in a siding and 75A Brighton based 41303 running light engine at Guildford. Certainly if the 4-SUB were working today the electric heaters underneath all of the seats would keep the passengers very warm indeed, and all the trodden in slush and snow would turn the compartments into saunas. The steam heat appears to be effective back along the carriages behind Drummond Class T9, 30724 as it wheezes away from Brookwood in March 1955. *Both: Colour Rail*

Fresh from a general overhaul here within the works at Eastleigh in January, 1954 another of Drummond's fine Greyhounds gets a go on the depot's turntable before heading out on test. Most likely taken the same day was this view of Maunsell Class E1, 32697 awaiting a return somehow to its home shed of 72A Exmouth Junction and probable banking duties between Exeter St. Davids and Exeter Central. *Both: Colour Rail*

A chance for our cameraman to photograph Bulleid Pacifics in snow and sunshine should not be missed in December 1964, as a filthy 35019 French Line CGT strides across Setley Plain with steam to spare. *Colour Rail*

Opposite: Likewise an equally filthy 35016 Elders Fyffes heads in the opposite direction on the same bright winter's day in 1964. Both Merchant Navy Pacifics would be withdrawn in the coming New Year. *Colour Rail*

Also of interest from Strathwood to collect

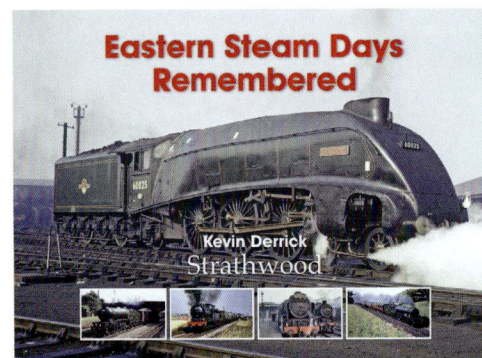

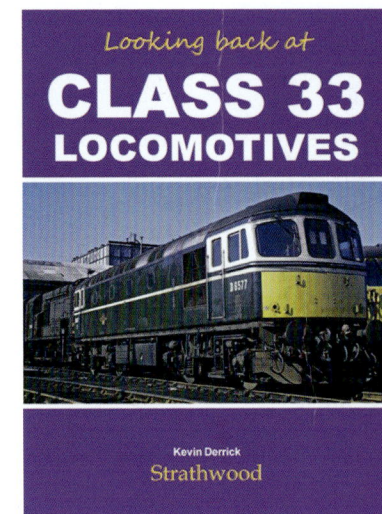

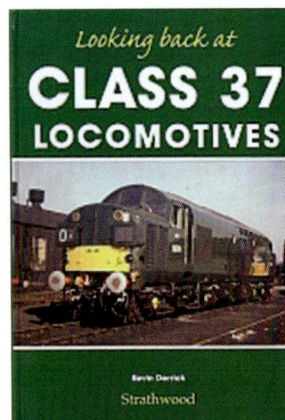

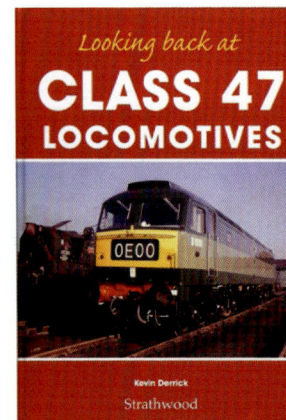